Introduction

As a teacher for decades, I have had an inside look at how education has turned against the foundations of American society. The demonization of Western Civilization started with calling Nationalism one of the four main causes of WWI. Western Civilization with Christianity as its foundation is the last great hope for a free world, so the opponents of freedom have deemed Christians the enemy of the state, domestic terrorists.

I used to teach American history to high school students and I, like most American high school teachers used the acronym M.A.I.N to teach the causes of WWI. M stands for militarism, A is for alliances, I is for imperialism, and N is for Nationalism. I did not realize then how this idea of nationalism would become such a tool for division.

When I attended school in the largest school district in Ohio I was extremely uncomfortable about the emphasis in many of my classes. Even though I have a very diverse bloodline, I am the color of "The Man" as we were called. I never have figured out exactly who "The Man" is but I guess it is any white person, especially one that is in charge. The emphasis in the minority-majority district during Black History Month spanning my attendance in middle school (at least) and continuing during the decades of teaching experience was to show how evil

America was and is. My sources say it has gotten worse in just a few years since I left the system.

In the 1990s, when teaching, I was not just "The Man" but a "Cracker" until students realized that I was their biggest advocate. But within my school building, I would listen in on other classes when I had a break. I would hear teachers teaching this very concept of "The Man" and how you can not trust white people.

White people were not the only target. Textbooks included the story of Genesis, however, this was taught in the Greek Mythology section of the book. This Bible book would be compared to other stories to demonstrate the Bible is just copy and pasting stories from other cultures, including the flood and Noah.

To make matters even worse, the books that were required reading materials were also about religion. The theme with these religious readings was to show that all religions are equal and valid.

Before the Scopes trial that effectively led to The Theory of Evolution being taught as science, the Bible story of Creation was seen as valid and respected. Macroevolution is now taught in public schools as if it is fact, even though it is called a theory. The fact that macro-evolution is considered a theory when it does not qualify as a theory, is just incredible or laughable. This "theory" is considered the "atheist Bible" to many.

The discarding of the Bible and prayer in schools took a couple of well known court-cases ***Abington School District v. Schempp*** and ***Engel v. Vitale.*** The secular-humanists have gained control of the government schools, and in many cases private schools as well. Education in America is near complete, if not almost entirely secular-humanistic, and is clearly anti-western and effectively anti-America as secular humanists intended.

The focus of this short-read book is to demonstrate how the dominos are falling into place as many intended. One way to destroy the most successful country in the history of the world is to cut away at its foundations, making the belief in this foundational underpinning subject to being deemed "Domestic Terrorists."

The Decline of Western Civilization

The Book that Made Your World: How the Bible Created the Soul of Western Civilization by Indian scholar Vishal Mangalwadi says all you need to know in his title. Unfortunately, some forces are successfully weakening the foundations and gains Western Civilization has made.

Mangalwadi 's book assesses the Bible as creating fertile ground for women to find social and economic empowerment, uniquely equipping the West to cultivate compassion, human rights, prosperity, and strong families. Vishal Mangalwadi highlights history in a cross-cultural manner demonstrating the many benefits of biblical principles in shaping civilization.

In general, Western culture has become increasingly secular-humanistic in Europe and America for many years. The strong Catholic influence has diminished so much that the current Pope has been influenced by his Marxist homeland and his very liberal views on abortion and gay lifestyles have been shocking to many Catholics, including the popular Mother Miriam.

Thank America and the West for personal computers emerging and changing the world. Americans developed the World Wide Web revolutionizing global communications and linking the world as never before.

At first, the internet allowed free access to vast amounts of information, while outside the democratic West, the web contained information the totalitarian states would not let go uncensored and still do not.

Education was the Bible-based platform of education in America's early years, but over time, America and the rest of the West have succumbed to secular humanism.

Plato observed, "The direction in which education starts a man will determine his future in life." The Renaissance philosopher Erasmus stated, "The main hope of a nation lies in the proper education of its youth." In many ways schools are the most powerful institutions in our society.

Historically, leaders in early Western educational institutions were strong Christians believers and taught Christian values as learning fundamentals. But the Scopes trial helped pushed these believers and their beliefs to the curb.

Charles Darwin's *On the Origin of Species*, is now just referenced as "The Theory of Evolution" or "Darwinism." This theory has been very successful in creating doubts on the credibility of the Bible, the validity of Judeo-Christian moral principles, and the role of God as the Creator—foundational principles that had long been taught in European and American schools.

The Enlightenment of the 1700s began to grow and expand, and increasingly became a whipping board for the Catholic Church. The Catholic Church preferred the Geocentric Theory, which turned out to be wrong, Since the Geocentric Theory was deemed wrong it ushered in a loss of credibility to Christianity being reliable. Plus the Enlightenment thinkers are given all of the credit in government schools for shaping the US Constitution, dismissing the Judeo-Christian influence.

The majority of times Christianity is mentioned in a school setting, the Bible was used to promote slavery incorrectly. The real history is that some claimed to be Christians who did use the Bible incorrectly, however, it has been Christianity that has helped to end global slavery and dictatorship more than any other religion. Just because a group takes scriptures out of context to justify immorality, does not mean the Biblical principles are at fault.

John Dewey could be argued to be the "father" of progressive education. Working around the turn of the twentieth century, Dewey rejected the Bible and promoted secular-humanism via evolution, psychology, and socialism. He claims to have, like progressives/liberals today believe, a "morally superior" way of life.

Dewey followers replaced Godly moral absolutes of right and wrong and like today's Marxist-phallic educators focused on feelings and experience and dismissed the value of reading, writing, and those historical facts. Sound familiar? This has been incremental, but now it is now approaching light speed.

In the 1930s, Marxist intellectuals from Frankfurt's Institute for Social Research fled Germany and gained power in liberal American universities, where they devised cultural Marxism programs, creating a cultural revolution to undermine Western capitalism and "outmoded" **Biblical** values and bringing about a utopian socialist society. Christian values of family and morals, individual freedoms, and private property had to be destroyed.

The goal of the Marxists was to gain control of the schools and eliminate the use of the Bible and Christianity. They wanted to break up the family, upending traditional gender roles for men and women, and discrediting foundational elements of Western history and civilization in the name of multi-culturalism. They wanted to redefine tolerance.

The former understanding of tolerance when I was growing up was Voltarian, which stated "I may not agree with what you say, but I will defend to death you right to say it." Whereas tolerance today is very eclectic in that it states that one must believe what someone else believes or they are considered intolerant.

These Marxist ideas from the 1930s have permeated educational institutions in America and the West after helping create student radicals of the '60s who are now teachers, administrators, judges, media writers, actors, film producers, politicians, and the technology we all depend on.

Freedom of speech and thought has been recreated into this Orwellian nightmare. Now word meanings are hard to keep up with, "trigger words" and "microaggressions" are invented daily. Words that might seem pro-Western are ridiculed and even suppressed.

The results have been scary. Freedom of speech is being redefined daily by government institutions and the Marxist sympathizing social media companies. Conservatives are being silenced or kicked out of the most influential media platforms and government positions.

Radical activist professors become prominent rewriting about the success in the West and making foolish claims that ignore the accomplishments focusing on negative history, disproportionately narratives of oppression, exploitation, and extermination.

Students today have been conditioned to hate and ignore the one source that prophesized what is happening in the modern Western world: the Bible. Biblical scholars see these prophecies as playing out in these last days. Misguided leaders help take people away from God and His word. "Those who lead you cause you to err" Isaiah 3:12, calling good "evil" and evil "good" in Isaiah 5:20.

<h1 style="text-align:center">Lebanon vs America</h1>

I believe in the Venn diagram concept of learning. Often the truth lies somewhere in the middle. Although triangulating the truth would even be better.

I will start by offering the perspective of the left. The Atlantic published an article by Kim Ghattas which stated:

" If you think the Middle East has always been as it is today, you are mistaken: There lies in the not-so-distant past a more vibrant, diverse, colorful, calm, tolerant the Middle East, not only one with no militias or beheadings, but one with progress, hope, and development. Before there were killings over apostasy charges, there were public debates between secular and religious Muslim thinkers, attended by hundreds. Those who stood up for freedom of thought and expression, who critiqued the role of religion in politics, were many, and their critics were few. Over time, the numbers didn't necessarily change, but the balance of power did, and liberal thinkers were cowed by the violence that fanatics were willing to deploy."

Ms. Ghattas goes on to assert that America is basically in the same transition from a free country that loved diversity to a country of fanatics. Ghattas blames Donald Trump for exacerbating the fanatical mindset in America.

Brigitte Gabriel, well-known Islamic expert, author and speaker's assessment about Lebanon is similar, with a major exception. Gabriel explains how radical Muslims took over her homeland of Lebanon and legislated their religious morality to be in line with Islamic radicalism.

When explaining the global threat she explained: "There are 1.2 billion Muslims in the world, 180-to-300 million are dedicated to the destruction of Western civilization, even though, of course, most Muslims are not radical."

Gabriel added that the peaceful majority were irrelevant because, for instance, 19 Muslims were responsible for September 11th. Gabriel went on to compare 'peaceful' Muslims to Germans during the Nazi regime, saying that "most Germans were peaceful, yet the Nazis drove the agenda and as a result, 60 million died." To suggest otherwise, she later added, was political correctness that should be thrown in the garbage.

Gabriel went on to say:

"The elected officials of the state should not try changing the public morality by legislative/judicial means to achieve the political goals they failed to achieve in the course of democratic elections – the political goals that are incompatible with the established public morality of a country. Unfortunately, that is what is going on these days in the USA and Israel, and many Jews are the active participants in these destructive political activities."

Brigitte Gabriel hit home with this statement, "My past is America's future unless America wakes up today and understands why it is so important to preserve our national identity."

So, we have major divisions in America. The left blames Donald Trump (and ostensibly his followers), while the conservative's viewpoint is that the left radicals are the real problem.

The mainstream media controls close to 90 percent of the school children still attending government schools, the largest social media platforms, the colleges and universities, and the mainstream media. Besides talk-radio, the conservative viewpoint is almost non-existent.

The fact that American information flow is controlled by the left, and now has given the lead to the far-left Marxists, those that love America's founding principles have reasonable concerns. The only real question for those that appreciate Western Civilization is if there is yet time to stop America from becoming more like Lebanon and China.

Christianity is the Pillar of American Society

As a teacher, I found it saddening when my fellow history teachers took the path of negative history and refused to acknowledge the value of Christianity in American history. Although their omission is understandable given the fact that I attended a Christian College and astoundingly did not have much taught about Christianity's value either.

Christianity is vital to understanding American culture. **John Adams** explained, "The Bible contains the most profound philosophy, the most perfect morality, and the most refined policy that ever was conceived upon earth." We sure miss morality in schools and daily life.

John Quincy Adams said, "The Bible is the best of all books in the world that which contributes most to make men good, wise, and happy." The Bible is comforting, historical, and teaches us to love even our enemies.

Thomas Jefferson made the point, "The doctrines of Jesus are simple, and tend all to the happiness of man. … Had the doctrines of Jesus been preached always as pure as they came from his lips, the whole civilized world would now have been Christian."

Leading Atheist, Richard Dawkins saw the moral decline of world society and had to admit that the world's rejection of God's existence has led us here. He even said that it would continue, and in this case, he is correct.

America and globally society has forces working diligently to dismantle what is left of Western Civilization, and the foundation is grounded in Christianity. According to Wikipedia, "Christianity has been intricately intertwined with the history and formation of Western Society." There is no doubt about the influence of Christianity.

Alexis de Tocqueville had this to say:

"Democracy extends the sphere of individual freedom, socialism restricts it. Democracy attaches all possible value to each man; socialism makes each man a mere agent, a mere number. Democracy and socialism have nothing in common but one word: equality. But notice the difference: while democracy seeks equality in liberty, socialism seeks equality in restraint and servitude. Americans are so enamored of equality, they would rather be equal in slavery than unequal in freedom. Nothing is more wonderful than the art of being free, but nothing is harder to learn how to use than freedom. Liberty cannot be established without morality, nor morality without faith."

Besides acknowledging the historical debt that political freedom we all owe to Christianity, de Tocqueville also expressed that a free society necessarily requires a religious foundation. He is absolutely correct.

Where The Left Get Their Marching Orders

America is without-a-doubt amidst transition. When a Democratic Party Candidate can proudly run as a socialist in America, you realize times have changed dramatically. The Democratic Party of JFK is gone. This is the party of the radical left, at least for now.

The Democrat Party's initiatives are parroting the admitted Marxist organization called BLM (Black Lives Matter). BLM's worldview is based on the antithesis of Christianity. The organization and ideology focus on the external, pushing two wild "theories" that are gaining traction in government schools: which include **Critical race theory and Intersectional theory**.

Critical Race Theory claims that racism is systemic, based on a system of white supremacy, and therefore a permanent feature of American life.

The intersectional theory claims that people are often disadvantaged and oppressed because of their race, class, gender identity, sexual orientation, religion, and many other LGBTQ identifications.

Black Lives Matter and supporters of critical race theory and intersectional theory do not believe in individual responsibility for crimes since, according to them, blacks are systemic and permanent victims of racism.

BLM believes the racism and white power structure (Western Civilization) can only be defeated by destroying the American economic, political and social system and rebuilding it from scratch, and replacing our ways with Marxist principles.

The BLM website states their Goals: 1) abolish the Judeo-Christian concept of the traditional nuclear family, the basic social unit in America; 2) abolish the police and dismantle the prison system; 3) mainstream transgenderism and delegitimize so-called heteronormativity (the belief that heterosexuality is the norm), and 4) abolish capitalism (a free economy) and replace it with communism (a government-controlled economy).

BLM leaders have threatened to "burn down the system" if their demands are not met. They are also training militias.

President Trump wanted Antifa labeled as a terrorist group, however Trump said very little about the much more slippery-slope of addressing BLM.

BLM and Antifa are not very far apart ideologically, according to expert Andy Ngo. Ngo states in his book <u>Unmasked</u>:

"Simply put, Antifa is an ideology and movement of radical pan-leftist politics whose adherents are mainly militant anarchist communists or collectivist anarchists. A smaller fraction of them are socialists who organize through political groups like the Democratic Socialists of America and others. Labels aside, their defining characteristics are a militant opposition."

Antifa and BLM are in reality radicals mentioned and celebrated by the left. Hillary Clinton and Barack Obama, two of the leaders for the left are still leaving their progressive mark and remain influential well after their terms in office. Both Clinton and Obama were (and I presume still are) clearly influenced by Neo-Marxist Saul Alinsky's book <u>Rules for Radicals.</u>

Former Senator Clinton quoted Alinsky in her Political Science Thesis. For example, she quoted from Alinksy's book, "America's radicals are to be found wherever and whenever America moves close to the fulfillment of its democratic dream. Whenever America's hearts are breaking, there American radicals were and are. America was begun by its radicals. America was built by its radicals. The hope and future of America lies with its radicals." Its apparent radicals, to Clinton, are necessary and bring positive change.

"Obama learned his lesson well. I am proud to see that my father's model for organizing is being applied successfully beyond local community organizing to affect the Democratic campaign in 2008. It is a fine tribute to Saul Alinsky as we approach his 100th birthday." --Letter from Saul's son, David Alinsky. Obama not only taught principles from Alinsky, he acted on them.

Obama's friend and supporter that helped Obamaget elected was none other than the radical terrorist, William Ayers. Sean Hannity, a host on Fox News, spent a lot of time hammering on these facts about Obama, but the main-stream media (MSM) dismissed this (like Alinsky teaches) so much that it never gained any traction.

Clinton nor Obama are necessarily giving orders for BLM or Antifa, however I noticed that neither spoke out against the chaos and destruction both Marxist groups have perpetuated over the last several years.

So, who gives the left their marching orders? Key players: Ocasio-Cortez , Rep. Ilhan Omar of Minnesota, Rep. Mark Pocan of Wisconsin, Rep. Ayanna Pressley of Massachusetts, Rep. Rashida Tlaib of Michigan, Bill de Blasio, Sen. Jeff Merkley of Oregon, Bernie Sanders, Elizabeth Warren, Stacey Abrams, Cory

Booker, Pete Buttigieg, Julian Castro, Kamala Harris, Jay Inslee, and Beto O'Rourke, to name a few.

CNN believes via coverage, the "Squad," led by AOC, is the most powerful group ready to replace the older generation, paving the way for radical Marxism, just the way Alinsky would like it. The marching orders of the left come from the playbooks derived from Alinsky and Marx.

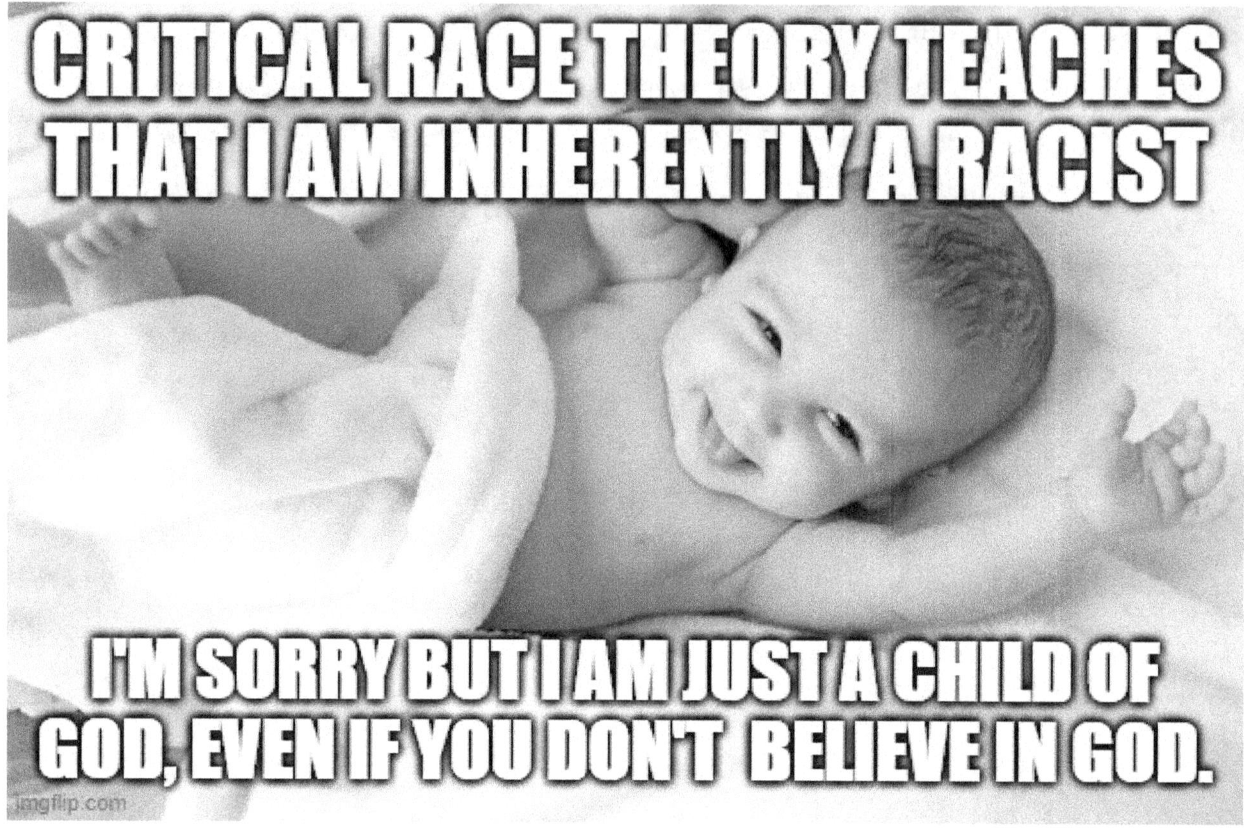

An outgrowth of the European Marxist school of critical theory, critical race theory is an academic movement that seeks to link racism, race, and power.

Anti-racists must find these "implicit biases" in all aspects of life, ranging from discussions in the classroom to interactions between colleagues.

To ensure greater equality of outcome, several universities have taken steps to make their admissions processes more "equitable." These actions can range from scrapping standardized tests to in many cases adding a diversity or equity scorecard to applications. This would not be such a bad idea if students did not see this as a way out of valuing learning.

Teachers are not big fans of standardized testing or teaching to-the-test, but the idea of eliminating all standardized tests goes too far. The ACT, for example, is a test that triple-dips as an alternate state test, placement into college honors courses, and opportunity for scholarships.

To get the "white staff and students" to understand their "implicit biases," institutions have forced us to undergo some form of training throughout each teaching year. White teachers must agree to their inherent racism or face consequences.

Universities advocates have been pushing for changes in the undergraduate curriculum, ranging from a mandatory class on anti-racism to forcing instructors to embed anti-racist ideology in their class material. Academic freedom is gone. The codes of conduct now include incomprehensible language on "hate speech" and "racist language," the Marxist sympathizers revel in.

Corporations have chosen political sides by donating money to the same organizations that have ties to Antifa and BLM and encouraged students to get involved in these politically anti-Christian groups. Big dollars are being used to fund Critical Race Theory.

In response to campus protests, university administrators have taken steps to either disarm or defund their police departments, often replacing them with unarmed officers or mental health workers.

Remember President Obama's statement, "They get bitter, they cling to guns or religion or antipathy to people who aren't like them or anti-immigrant sentiment or anti-trade sentiment as a way to explain their frustrations." Now the marching orders are in.

Bill Clinton just so happened to pardon a member of the Weather Underground that is now helping finance BLM, Susan Rosenberg. Universities have provided books like *How to be an Antiracist* and *White Fragility* free for students and started anti-racist "action committees" or renamed what they deem offensive buildings names to oblige the demands of the far left.

Miguel Cardona, President-elect Joe Biden's education secretary nominee, recently oversaw the creation of (soon-to-be mandated) critical race theory courses for high schoolers in Connecticut. Biden also rescinded a Trump-era order that banned training that implies anyone is racist or sexist "under his or her race, sex, and/or national origin." Now the Christian and white hate sentiment can continue at the federal level once again.

A mailing was given to parents in NYC so the white parents could convert themselves to the best whites can be, "white traitors." Students will be forced into submission to tolerate Critical Race Theory to guilt some while empowering others into believing government is the only saving grace.

The Bible is not a white religion even if you believe there is such thing as a

white race. The Bible teaches there are two groups of people "Believers or

Unbelievers." The idea of race is a social construct used as a tool to divide that has been used to promote evolution to substantiate its flawed reasoning.

The New Yorker's article American Christianity's *White-Supremacy Problem* claimed that, "Nearly two-thirds of white Christians overall said that killings of African-American men by the police are isolated incidents rather than part of a broader pattern of mistreatment." In other words, if you don't bow down and agree with the premise that cops, (especially white cops) are inherently racists, then your lack of belief that cops are all racists means that you must be racist.

Keep in mind the new narrative is that whites must accept that they are inherently racist. Remember when former President Obama said, " the legacy of slavery, Jim Crow, discrimination in almost every institution of our lives — you know, that casts a long shadow. And that's still part of our DNA that's passed on. We're not cured of it." Obama gave the hints of what was to come.

NPR posted an article entitled, *White Supremacist Ideas Have Historical Roots In U.S. Christianity* to make the transition from white supremacists to Christians as the tool or justification for racism. Here is an excerpt:
"Some Christian theologians went so far as to argue that the enslavement of human beings was justifiable from a Biblical point of view. James Henley Thornwell, a Harvard-educated scholar who committed huge sections of the Bible to memory, regularly defended slavery and promoted white supremacy from his pulpit at the

First Presbyterian Church in Columbia, S.C., where he was the senior pastor in the years leading up to the Civil War." This is revisionist history.

Robert P. Jones, author of *White Too Long: The Legacy of White Supremacy in American Christianity* claims, "Over the last several weeks, the United States has engaged in a long-overdue reckoning with the racist symbols of the past, tearing down monuments to figures complicit in slavery and removing Confederate flags from public displays. But little scrutiny has been given to the cultural institutions that legitimized the worldview behind these symbols: **white Christian churches**."

Jones takes the stance of NPR to the next step. NPR portrayed the Southern Christians were using the Bible as a tool to justify slavery, and in effect portraying Christianity as the driver of the "white superiority complex."

Jones writes:

"A close read of history reveals that we white Christians have not just been complacent or complicit; rather, as the nation's dominant cultural power, we have constructed and sustained a project of perpetuating white supremacy that has framed the entire American story. The legacy of this unholy union still lives in the DNA of white Christianity today — and not just among white evangelical Protestants in the South, but also white mainline Protestants in the Midwest and white Catholics in the Northeast."

So, there you have it, Christianity is the tool to oppress. Christianity is the facilitator of racism. Therefore, Christians are racists. Leading to Christianity is the the "white religion" or the religion of "sell-outs" or "Uncle Toms."

Uncle Tom's

One might falsely believe that the goal for leftists and Marxists is to stamp out Christian whites, since that has seemed to have been the primary enemy for several decades, at least. But closer attention to detail will help you understand that race-baiting is just a smokescreen.

An Uncle Tom is someone who "sold out and embraced the white man by rejecting the idea that you're a victim," according to radio host Larry Elder. Black men have been called 'Uncle Toms' from Dr. Martin Luther King, Jr. to former president Barack Obama, at some point, they were accused of being too passive or a sell-out to the race.

"The concept of the sellout Uncle Tom, however, is characterized by the idea of a Black man who appears only interested in serving whites, the government, corporations, or 'the system' generally. The insult is meant to connote that these men, these 'Uncle Toms' will ensure that white needs come before the needs of both the Black community and themselves," explains Cheryl Thompson, writing for The National Interest.

Selling out to whites can be as simple as allowing depictions of a white Jesus since a white Jesus raises concerns about racism, according to Terry Mattingly of the Knoxville News Sentinel. I wonder when Jesus is depicted as Asian in countries like South Korea whether that would be considered racist? I doubt it.

Politically, Joe Biden, the self-proclaimed leader of the left recently stated, "If you have a problem figuring out whether you're for me or Trump then you ain't black." Joe believes Blacks need to stay in their box (only supporting Democrats). Otherwise Joe and many of his followers might call Trump supporters "Uncle Toms."

Candace Owens jokes that the most ridiculous name she has been called is "a Black-white supremacist." Candace is a well-known Christian Conservative. "White supremacy and white nationalism is not a problem that is harming black America," Owens said in a congressional hearing. Candace was bold, calling on the African-American community to start "putting fathers back in the home and demanding a return to God, religion, and shrinking government."

Students in one Philadelphia elementary school were allegedly forced to celebrate "black communism" and endure a mock Black Power rally to "free" Angela Davis, outspoken radical political activist, from "jail." The indoctrination to Marxist principles is no longer a hidden agenda but forced into student submission.

Shelby Steele is a Civil Rights leader from Chicago that learned from teaching in St. Louis, the poorest neighborhood in the country at the time. He realized that what is killing the Black community is liberalism. *What Killed Michael Brown?* is Steele's documentary that argues LBJ's Great Society liberalism laid the foundation for 2014's police killing of Michael Brown in Ferguson, Missouri.

Steele writes, "What killed Michael Brown is the liberalism that put him in public housing, that expanded welfare payments so that his family broke up, the fatherless home, the terrible education, terrible schools, terrible public housing, uh, the destructive school busing." Steele is in agreement with Candace Owens.

Dr. Steele says where Blacks need help is exactly the opposite of what the Marxists are teaching. Biblical parenthood and Churches should be leading the Black culture, not the government. Marxists emphasize and encourage the break-up of family and destruction of "organized (Christian) religion." Steele says, "Nihilism, the rejection of all religious and moral principles, in the belief that life is meaningless, is the problem, not the solution."

Dr. Steele claims Blacks attend the worst schools in the world, yet the liberals, many Marxist sympathizers are in control of most of the education in government schools and universities. The influence of the anti-Western, anti-Biblical teaching is taught from preschool to adulthood, on cable news, social media, and just about every form of information except the dwindling memberships of churches and radio programs.

Dr. Steele recognizes he is seen as an Uncle Tom, stating, "Any white who says these things is going to be seen as racist, and any black who says them is going to be seen as an Uncle Tom. That's because the only politically correct way to see blacks is as victims of larger forces that are constantly determining them and beating them and miring them in difficulty."

C. Gane McCalla, a writer for NewsOne, says liberal Juan Williams is an Uncle Tom since, "Although Williams cried after Obama's election, he has returned to his sell-out ways. He called Michelle Obama Stokely Carmichael in a designer dress and has done nothing to speak up against Fox's racism." Blacks are not allowed to criticize Democrats or anyone from the left's perspective or risk the Uncle Tom label.

Star Parker, author of Uncle Sam's Plantation said about the liberal tactics, "So, following the advice of Alinsky, they get attention not by developing quality ideas for public policy reform and engaging in thoughtful discourse about these ideas, but through sensational hype of dogma and character assassination of those who disagree. Parker is spot-on.

As a result, the discussion is not about the merits of the socialism they are selling, about their big-government answers to health, housing, education, and lifting the poor, but about answering their charges that anyone who does not agree with them is a racist." Hence calling those that disagree racist or Uncle Tom is the best way to shut down the opposition.

The race-card is the oldest trick in the book to silence critics and push agendas. Christopher F. Rufo, a writer from City Journal said, "The teachers' union openly demands that the United States overthrow the racist structure of capitalism, provide "reparations for Black and Indigenous people, and uproot white supremacy and plant the seeds for a new world."

Recently Coach Flynn, a well-liked football coach that had rebuilt his hometown team by dedicating his life to his players and gave a substantial amount of his time on the field but also provides rides and equipment to players in need. was fired. The coach is supportive of all members of the community. He invited a female student to join the JV football team and welcomed a student with special

needs to serve as a team manager.

Coach Flynn was fired for question the Marxist BLM curriculum his

children were being taught. The district Superintendent explained, "significant

philosophical differences," caused the firing. This is the same line schooll districts

use for most of their firings. Marxists hate American values because we are

granted freedom of expression.

In conclusion, the labeling of being called an Uncle Tom is proof that "the

man" is not just a white man, but whomever does not bow down to the ideological

Marxist, the left. The Marxists are using the race-card to push their agenda.

The FBI lists the Domestic Terrorist Categories as sovereign citizens, abortion extremists, animal rights and environmental, military, anarchy, militia, and White supremacy extremists. The Southern Poverty Law Center (SPLC) clearly influences who makes the list.

So, where do the media and the left get their labels from? Largely the SPLC. This organization is the gold standard for legitimizing hatred of conservatives groups, including American Family Radio, a Christian broadcast company.

SPLC gets into the government classrooms by Teaching Tolerance, a curriculum that recommends educators talk about tolerance "as a basic American value, talk about it early, talk about it often, and talk about it in a lot of different contexts so that when the context does seem a little bit political, it's part of a bigger picture." Of course, tolerance does not mean tolerate, it means vocally to make it clear you agree with the current deviant cause or anti-Christian perspective without question or be called a racist or some "ism."

Teaching Tolerance has a website, Tolerance.org, which is kind enough to give props to a former and a proud domestic terrorist founder, Bill Ayers. The SPLC's Mark Potok, said, "Sometimes the press will describe us as monitoring hate groups, I want to say plainly that our aim in life is to destroy these groups, destroy them."

In email correspondence, the FBI has admitted to working with the SPLC, said Mr. Gaetz in the July 23 letter, "This is surprising and worrisome, as the SPLC is known to use its platform in order to denigrate and disparage certain groups by labeling them 'hate groups.'" SPLC works with social media giants, Facebook and Twitter to identify "hate groups."

Who are the terrorists? Whomever the SPLC says are the terrorists.

The Last Terrorists

Take it from one of the most circulated papers in America, Christian

Nationalists are domestic terrorists. Unpack the loose definitions of Christian

Nationalists, and what do you get?

Rachel S. Mikva writes in USA Today, **Christian Nationalism** *is a threat,*

and not just from Capitol attackers invoking Jesus:

"It is a long-term strategy articulated decades ago by a leader in the Christian

Reconstructionist movement, Gary North. He argued that Christians must use the

doctrine of religious liberty to advance their agenda, hoping to raise children who

know that there is no religious neutrality, no neutral law, no neutral education, and

no neutral civil government. Then they will get busy in constructing a Bible-based

social, political, and religious order which finally denies the religious liberty of the enemies of God. The Christian right has embraced this approach in multiple court cases and bills, distorting the very meaning of religious freedom." This article is referring to the Capitol riot on January 6, 2021.

Mikva needed to expose her disdain for Christianity even more by using Ted Cruz as an example of Christians trying to use coded language when he, and Christians in general, use the phrase, "restoring America." To Mikva, and many with the far-left mindset, Cruz is, "Trying to hide the attempt to take over every aspect of society with religious themes." I must have missed this memo on the "Christian Coding."

What is Christian nationalism? Here are a few examples of the definitions being thrown around.

- "It's a deep emotional attachment to a particular and exclusive culture, a skewed version of history, and a false sense of 'marked superiority' that must and will fade away."

- "A collection of myths, traditions, symbols, narratives, and value systems — that idealizes and advocates a fusion of Christianity with American civic life…It includes assumptions of nativism, white supremacy, patriarchy, and heteronormativity, along with divine sanction for authoritarian control and militarism. It is as ethnic and political as it is religious."

- "Christian and American identities, are distorting both the Christian faith and America's constitutional democracy. Christian nationalism demands Christianity be privileged by the State and implies that to be a good American, one must be Christian. It often overlaps with and provides cover for white supremacy and racial subjugation.

According to Bruce Ashford, author of <u>One Nation Under God</u>, "Patriotism lapses into nationalism when your nation becomes your god or your functional savior. Nationalism supplants Christianity." I have never met folks that take their nation above God, but I have met plenty of people that take their political party above God.

Anthea Butler, author of the article, *White Evangelicals*, says, "Don't just condemn Christian nationalism, own it." Butler is the interim chair of Religious Studies and associate professor of religion and Africana studies at the University of Pennsylvania. Professor Butler makes it clear that Christians must bow down to the mob's newest mentality.

Professor Butler complained, "The Southern Baptist Convention has spent considerable time in the past year condemning **critical race theory**, first with a resolution at their 2019 annual meeting and most recently with a statement from six Southern Baptist seminary presidents proclaiming that the theory is incompatible with the denomination's statement of faith." Professor Butler is yet another Ivy Leaguer pushing the far-left agenda that forces compliance.

Politico mentions Elizabeth Neumann, a former top official at the Department of Homeland Security under Trump in their article, *It's Time to Talk About Violent Christian Extremism,* where she is adamant that:

" QAnon's popularity among certain segments of Christendom not as an aberration, but as the troubling-but-natural outgrowth of a strain of American Christianity. In this tradition, one's belief is based less on scripture than on conservative culture, some political disagreements are seen as having nigh-apocalyptic stakes and a strong authoritarian streak runs through the faith. For this type of believer, love of God and love of country are sometimes seen as the same. Christian nationalism is a huge theme throughout evangelical Christendom."

The Democrat Party and its Marxists have identified a new target for their wrath: "Christian Nationalists." They are redefining those words to be used in a deprecating context. The Left is setting up a straw man to take down all Christians.

There is an effort to redefine Christian nationalism by those who detest both Christians and Patriotism. Christian hatred is so easily understood by searching David Barton, easily one of the best historians of all time. His resources of artifacts and historical documents along with his ability to make the material understandable are second to none. I say this as a certified Social Studies teacher.

A David Barton internet search will lead you to articles that blast David for pointing out the American founding was built on Christian ideology. Barton has the research to prove it, but like anyone the left hates, he is dismissed as being a fake or right-wing hack. It is very difficult to find a site with one positive word to say about this historian.

Barton loves America and wants Americans to understand the Christian foundation, just as Alex de Tocqueville famously described. The Marxists realize their enemy, God and religion as the foundation of the West, and the enemy of the left that must have their influence removed.

President Barack Obama famously said, "American is not a Christian country." Leftists have been rewriting history for many years, set out to prove this to be a new truth. If they really believed this they should not need to spend so much time redefining historical facts to prove their faulty premise.

Christian Nationalism to the left is said to overlap with and provides cover for white supremacy and racial subjugation. No doubt the left's target list is a much broader round-up of those with whom it disagrees or whomever the disgraced SPLC has defined as the latest hate group.

The activist group (Christians) *Against Christian Nationalism* states, "Christian nationalism seeks to merge Christian and American identities, distorting both the Christian faith and America's constitutional democracy…As Christians, we must speak in one voice condemning Christian nationalism as a distortion of the gospel of Jesus and a threat to American democracy." Let me point out, that we are a Republic, not a democracy.

In the last days Christians, like *Against Christian Nationalism's* members, will be in rebellion with the word of God. Recently, a church in Tennessee made news by claiming the Bible is fallible, and not the only word of God. There are some within Christian spheres undermining the Christian message and validity.

Recently, Pastor Robert Jeffress, spoke the truth about what Christian Nationalism is: "God's no respecter of people or nations. But any nation that honors God will be blessed by God and any nation, including the United States of America, that rejects God will be rejected by God."

"And can the liberties of a nation be thought secure when we have removed their only firm basis, a conviction in the minds of the people that these liberties are the gift of God? That they are not to be violated but with His wrath? Indeed I tremble for my country when I reflect that God is just: that his justice cannot sleep forever." —Thomas Jefferson (1781)

The notion that God had a uniquely Christian purpose for our country pretty well sums up the views of our Founding Fathers, the same men the left want to destroy and tear down any reference about them. The idea that if there are skeletons or flaws in life are the excuse to dismiss the formation of the greatest and most diverse and unique country is at least absurd but definitely foolish.

The Christian Nationalism label is the latest attempt to silence believers. **Christian Nationalism** is the latest evolution of "the man." Now the Marxists have finally put their real enemy in sight: **Christians**.

Andy Ngo, February 22, 2021 posted on Telegram, "The deadly assault of an elderly American man in San Francisco is being blamed on white nationalism by left-wing activists. Antoine Watson, the suspect arrested over the homicide is black." There is a flyer for a 2PM protest later that same week.

What's even crazier is what recently was proposed in the U.S. Congress. Illinois Representative Brad Schneider's proposed bill, H.R. 350 that is overkill for even the former Democratic Presidential nominee Tulsi Gabbard. Gabbard believes, "the new 'Domestic Terrorism' Bill could target pro-life Christians and almost half of the country."

Congresswoman Gabbard explained why the HR 350 is a dangerous bill: "What characteristics are we looking for as we are building this profile of a potential extremist? What are we talking about?" Gabbard raised, "Religious extremists, are we talking about Christians, evangelical Christians? What is a religious extremist? Is it somebody who is pro-life? Where do you take this?"

Christianity is the enemy of Marxism, the enemy of slavery, and the enemy of the elite. The left have implored the "Never let a tragedy go to waste," as the strategy to fundamentally change America since the very day they were given notice.

Christians understand that we are in the End Times. And in the end, Christians are the latest, and the last hope for freedom, and therefore the last domestic terrorists, soon, if the Marxists on the left get their way.

Citations

https://news.americanbible.org/blog/entry/corporate-blog/6-quotes-about-the-bible-from-the-founding-fathers

https://www.intellectualtakeout.org/blog/its-america-save-western-civilization/

https://en.wikipedia.org/wiki/Role_of_Christianity_in_civilization

https://bookroo.com/quotes/alexis-de-tocqueville#:~:text=%E2%80%9CIn%20America%20religion%20is%20the,leads%20man%20to%20civil%20freedom.%E2%80%9D

https://www.heritage.org/civil-society/report/tocqueville-christianity-and-american-democracy

https://www.goodreads.com/author/quotes/465.Alexis_de_Tocqueville

http://www.backboneamerica.net/america/2019/7/13/know-our-enemy-or-lose-our-liberty

https://crossexamined.org/what-if-god-is-removed-from-the-american-equation/

https://blogs.timesofisrael.com/religion-is-a-backbone-of-our-morality-and-society/

https://www.theatlantic.com/politics/archive/2014/06/video-benghazi-panel-turns-ugly-after-muslim-woman-asks-about-peaceful-muslims/372920/

https://www.youtube.com/watch?v=NWqVef1oiJw&ab_channel=CentennialInstitu
te

https://www.tomorrowsworld.org/magazines/2020/july-august/misguided-
education-and-the-decline-of-western-civilization

*The Book that Made Your World: How the Bible Created the Soul of Western
Civilization*

https://www.opendoorsusa.org/christian-persecution/

https://www.theatlantic.com/international/archive/2020/11/lessons-from-beirut-for-
america/616941/

https://www.actforamerica.org

https://www.dailymotion.com/video/x34olqe

http://www.backboneamerica.net/america/2019/7/13/know-our-enemy-or-lose-our-
liberty

https://www.israelunwired.com/brigitte-gabriel-reveals-the-muslim-plan-for-the-
destruction-of-america/

https://archives.fbi.gov/archives/news/stories/2008/november/hlf112508

https://faithandamericanhistory.wordpress.com/2016/08/12/tocqueville-on-
american-christianity-part-five-of-america-is-great-because-she-is-good/

Ngo, Andy. Unmasked (p. 13). Center Street. Kindle Edition.

Ngo, Andy. Unmasked (p. 92). Center Street. Kindle Edition.

Saul Alinsky's Rules for Radicals (crossroad.to)

http://hillsdalecollegian.com/2020/02/alumnus-exposes-corruption-of-splc-in-new-book-making-hate-pay/

https://en.wikipedia.org/wiki/History_of_Western_civilization

https://www.youtube.com/watch?v=dDeXhmTz_0M&ab_channel=eagfoundation

https://www.youtube.com/watch?v=AJ2LHgbDzqY&ab_channel=GlennBeck

https://criticalrace.org/what-is-critical-race-theory/

https://www.theguardian.com/world/2008/apr/14/barackobama.uselections2008

https://nypost.com/2020/12/23/biden-education-secretary-nominee-added-critical-theory-classes/

https://nypost.com/2021/01/24/biden-quietly-embraces-far-left-critical-race-theory/

https://cve.fbi.gov/whatare/?state=domestic

https://www.fbi.gov/cve508/teen-website/what-are-known-violent-extremist-groups

https://www.splcenter.org/hate-map?state=OH

The Gateway Pundit 2/16/202

https://www.influencewatch.org/non-profit/southern-poverty-law-center-splc/

https://www.newyorker.com/books/under-review/american-christianitys-white-supremacy-

problem?irclickid=2dWxjHz5wxyLU9GwUx0Mo3b2UkETUUwAEy2LWk0&irg
wc=1&source=affiliate_impactpmx_12f6tote_desktop_Bing%20Rebates%20by%2
0Microsoft&utm_source=impact-
affiliate&utm_medium=2003851&utm_campaign=impact&utm_content=Logo&ut
m_brand=tny

https://www.npr.org/sections/thetwo-way/2015/06/22/416476377/we-are-not-
cured-obama-discusses-racism-in-america-with-marc-maron

https://www.npr.org/2020/07/01/883115867/white-supremacist-ideas-have-
historical-roots-in-u-s-christianity

https://www.newsweek.com/uncle-tom-documentary-explores-what-its-like-
minority-within-minority-group-black-1493462

https://reason.com/podcast/2020/11/11/shelby-steele-what-really-killed-michael-
brown/

https://newsone.com/101141/top-5-fox-news-uncle-
toms/#:~:text=1%20Juan%20Williams.%20Despite%20the%20fact%20that%20W
illiams,4%20Angela%20McGlowan.%20...%205%20Erick%20Rush.%20

https://www.sfgate.com/entertainment/article/Shelby-Steele-has-a-lot-to-say-
about-black-2535245.php

https://www.theblaze.com/news/fifth-graders-forced-to-celebrate-black-
communism-hold-mock-black-power-rally-report

https://nationalinterest.org/blog/reboot/uncle-toms-cabin-still-impacts-racial-politics-today-177741

https://www.frc.org/updatearticle/20190731/christian-nationalism

https://www.nbcnews.com/think/opinion/racism-among-white-christians-higher-among-nonreligious-s-no-coincidence-ncna1235045

https://www.thedailybeast.com/candace-owens-to-congress-white-supremacy-and-white-nationalism-is-not-a-problem

https://www.usatoday.com/story/opinion/2021/01/31/christian-nationalism-josh-hawley-ted-cruz-capitol-attack-column/4292193001/

https://frenchpress.thedispatch.com/p/discerning-the-difference-between

https://www.christiansagainstchristiannationalism.org/statement

https://life1025.com/2016/06/the-fine-line-between-patriotism-and-nationalism/

https://religionnews.com/2020/12/14/white-evangelicals-dont-just-condemn-christian-nationalism-own-it/

https://www.politico.com/news/magazine/2021/02/04/qanon-christian-extremism-nationalism-violence-466034

https://www.dailywire.com/news/high-school-football-coach-fired-for-privately-questioning-black-lives-matter-curricula

https://patriotpost.us/alexander/65258-the-lefts-next-target-christian-nationalists-2019-09-04